Discover Sharks

HAMMERHEAD SHARK

Camilla de la Bédoyère

QED

QED Publishing

Copyright © QED Publishing 2012

First published in the UK in 2012 by
QED Publishing
A Quarto Group company
230 City Road
London EC1V 2TT

www.qed-publishing.co.uk

A catalogue record for this book is available from
the British Library.

ISBN 978 1 78171 072 2

Printed in China

Consultant Mary Lindeed
Editor Tasha Percy
Designer Melissa Alaverdy

Picture credits
Key: t = top, b = bottom,
m = middle, l = left, r = right

Alamy Norbert Probst 20-21, Stephen Frink
Collection 20bl
Ardea Valerie Taylor 4-5
FLPA Norbert Probst 10-11, Fred Bavendam/Minden
Pictures 12-13, 14-15, Tui De Roy/Minden Pictures 22-23
NHPA Charles Hood 1, 21b
OceanwideImages.com 16-17
Photoshot Jeremy Stafford-Deitsch/Oceans Image 6-7,
Charles Hood/Oceans Image 8-9, Charles Hood/
Oceans Image 24
Seapics.com 21t
Shutterstock michaeljung 2-3, Brandelet 18-19

Words in **bold** are explained in the Glossary on page 24

CONTENTS

WHAT IS A HAMMERHEAD?

A hammerhead is a **shark**. Its head looks like a hammer!

Sharks live in the ocean. They spend all their lives there.

We breathe in air.
Sharks breathe in water.

5

BIG BODY

This hammerhead
about 5 metres
ng. It is grey on
og. It is white

Fins help it to swim. Its
tail fin is long on the top
and short on the bottom.

tail fin

A STRANGE HEAD

eye

Look at the shark's head.
Can you find its eyes?

The shark's strange head
helps it to find animals
in the ocean. It also
helps the shark
to swim.

––––| eye

HUNGRY HUNTER

The hammerhead is ... ...roves its

It looks for animals to eat.
The shark knows when animals
are near, even when
it can't see them.

DINNERTIME

The hammerhead has
big teeth in its mouth.
It has about 25 teeth on the
top. It has about 25 teeth
on the bottom.

Hammerheads attack rays,
fish, squid, octopuses
and small sharks.

octopus

WARM OCEANS

Hammerhead sharks like to live in warm oceans. They swim where the water is not too deep.

They swim close to
the shore. They can
find lots of food there.

ON THE MOVE

Sharks are strong fish.
Their tails are full
of **muscles**. They can
swim very fast.

They sink to the
bottom of the ocean if
they stop swimming.

BABY SHARKS

Hammerheads can have up to **40** babies at a time! The babies are called **pups.**

A pup is about 60 centimetres long when it is born. It swims away from its mother and hunts for food.

pup

MORE HAMMERHEADS

There are different kinds of hammerhead sharks.

bonnethead

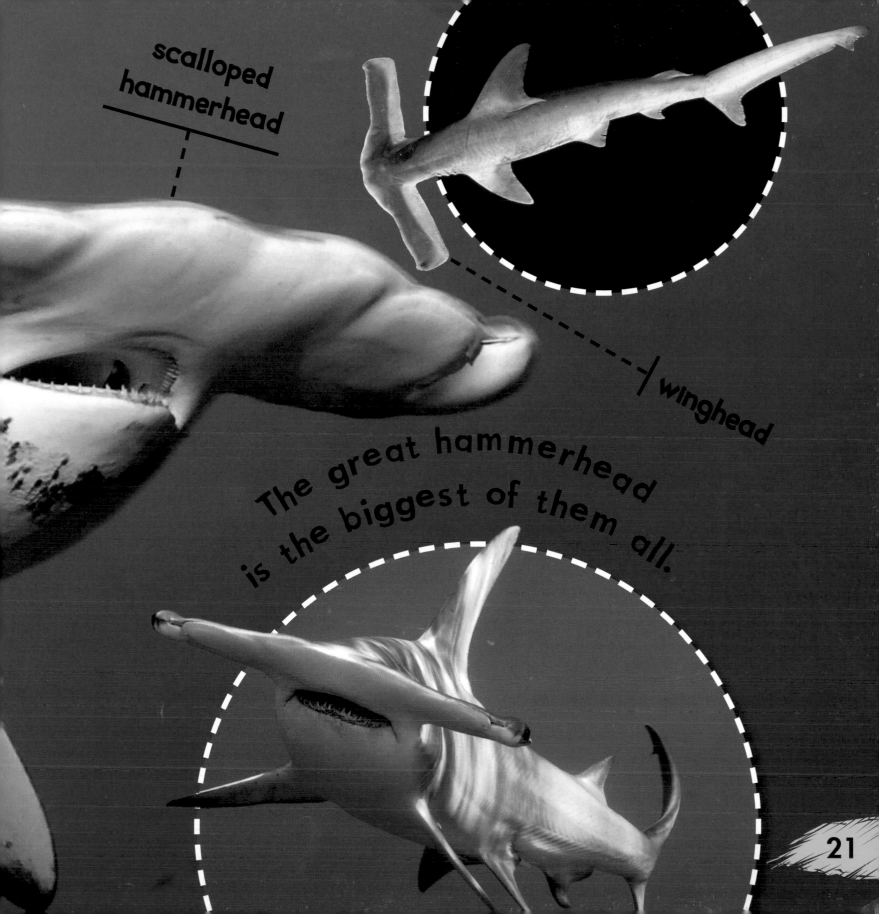

scalloped
hammerhead

winghead

The great hammerhead
is the biggest of them all.

21

Now we know that hammerhead sharks are amazing animals!

GLOSSARY

fin   a part on the body of a fish shaped like a flap, used for moving and steering through the water

fish   a cold-blooded animal that lives in water and has scales, fins and gills

muscle   a body part that produces movement by pulling on the bones to make them move

pup   a young shark

shark   a large and often fierce fish that feeds on meat and has very sharp teeth